IS EVERYTHING REALLY RELATIVE?

Examining the Assumptions of Relativism and the Culture of Truth *Decay*

☞ **W9-BZY-589**

Paul Copan

has a Ph.D. in philosophy from Marquette University in Milwaukee, Wisconsin. He has written *"True for You, But Not for Me": Deflating the Slogans That Leave Christians Speechless* (Bethany House) and has edited *Will the Real Jesus Please Stand Up?* (Baker). He is co-editor of a forthcoming book with InterVarsity Press. He has also contributed articles to *Trinity Journal, Dialogue,* and the *Christian Research Journal.* Paul works as a lecturer, writer, and researcher for Ravi Zacharias International Ministries in Norcross, Georgia. He lives with his wife Jacqueline and their five children—Johanna, Peter, Valerie, Erica, and Jonathan—in Suwanee, Georgia.

ISBN 1-930107-01-3

IS EVERYTHING REALLY RELATIVE?

Examining the Assumptions of Relativism and the Culture of Truth Decay

Paul Copan

Introduction

"It's all relative."
"That's just true for you, but not for me."
"Who are you to judge others?"
"How can you say you're right when so many people disagree?"
"Who are you to impose *your* morality on others?"
"That's just *your* reality.
"How can you say that your religion is the right one?"

These slogans have become so common in our society that to question them is to invite charges of arrogance and narrow-mindedness. The late philosopher and educator Allan Bloom wrote these now-famous words in *The Closing of the American Mind:* "There is one thing a professor can be absolutely sure of: almost every student entering the university believes, or says he believes, that truth is relative." A 1994 poll by the Barna Group revealed that 72% of American adults—that's almost 3 out of 4—affirmed some type of relativism. They agreed with the statement that there is "no such thing as absolute truth; two people could define truth in totally conflicting ways, but both still be correct."

That's what *relativism* is: A belief can be true for one person but not for another. "If you believe that Christianity is right for you, that's fine. I'm glad it works for you. I just happen to believe differently. But I'm not going to say that you're wrong," the relativist will declare. Clearly we live in an era of *truth* decay!

Now *why* is it that some people believe that relativism is true? Primarily because there are so many differing beliefs and opinions. So, we're often asked, isn't it really intolerant to think that one person or group of persons is right and others are wrong?

The idea of relativism has penetrated our society at many different levels—the university, the media, the workplace, and even religious institutions. As a result, those who believe that there are some fundamental or non-negotiable truths and moral values can feel intimidated about speaking their mind and voicing their convictions—no matter how kind and gracious their manner.

In his book *One Nation, After All*, Alan Wolfe of Boston University has documented how even religious people within America's middle class are reluctant to make any moral judgments. Any existing convictions about truth and morality appear to be caving in to the pressure of popular relativism. But to succumb to the pressures of a relativistic society is not only unnecessary; it is also the intellectually *inferior* position to hold. So the aim of this booklet is to show that (a) *no one can really be a relativist* and thus, contrary to popular belief, (b) *we are all absolutists to a significant extent*. And this is nothing to be ashamed of. Rather than being intimidated by a relativist, we can graciously offer good reasons for believing that absolutes such as "true" and "false" or "right" and "wrong" exist. We can resist this culture of truth decay.

But before we see the *inescapability* of truth, though, let's first say something about the *nature* of truth.

In Nick Park's delightful BBC children's film *A Grand Day Out*, Wallace, an inventor and cheese *aficionado*, tells his astonishingly intelligent dog Gromit that he wants to go to the moon for a vacation. The reason? Everyone knows that the moon is made of *cheese*. So they both set out to build a rocket ship, load it with plenty of crackers, and take off for an adventuresome grand day out. We smile because we know that *it isn't* true that the moon is made of cheese. That is, Wallace's belief doesn't *correspond or conform* to reality. What is true must correspond to reality; otherwise, it is false. Therefore if *truth* means anything at all, *it must exclude something*—namely, *falsehood.*[1]

This brings us to a very important question to consider: *Why do we believe the things we do?* The common answers to this question are—our culture, our parents, our religious upbringing, our psychological desires for purpose or comfort. But let's ask ourselves: "Do we think our beliefs are true *on this basis?*" Certainly not. After all, we may often reject certain beliefs of parents and friends or culture. We may often come to disagree with certain assumptions, prejudices, and beliefs drummed into us early in life. But *why* do we do this? The most likely answer is that we do not find everything we grew up with to be *true*—that is, corresponding to reality. For instance, someone may grow up in an environment of racial hatred but later on recognizes the intrinsic dignity of all human beings and embraces this truth.

So even though we may have embraced the beliefs of our parents and friends as well as various cultural assumptions, they are not necessarily *true*. (To take this view would be to commit the *genetic fallacy*—maintaining that a view is true—or false—simply because of its origin. For instance, I don't reject 2+2=4 as false just because I *disliked* the person who happened to teach it to me as a first-grader. Nor do I accept 2+2=5 as true because I *liked* the teacher who taught this erroneous bit of math—or because the teacher was an authority on *other* subjects.) In other words, factors such as family or culture may be the *causes or sources* of our beliefs, but they are still not *rational reasons* to accept those beliefs as true. So even if the sources of our beliefs are near and dear to us, we don't accept these beliefs as true *because* of this fact or *on the basis of* these influences. We may still freely reject beliefs from our upbringing because we later find them to be false.

It seems that people generally cannot function and flourish in a world that they *know* does not *correspond to reality*. (Such people end up being institutionalized!) If a person calls me a friend yet repeatedly insults me and mistreats me, I have good reason to disbelieve him. Why? I am inclined to form my belief on something more basic than my friend's word—namely, the *reality* of the situation. Of course, we'll often rationalize or try to explain things away if apparent contradictions exist between what we say we believe and what we are experiencing. But we find things falling apart in a hurry if we hold to beliefs we *know* are false. So it seems reasonable for us to *minimize* the false beliefs we have and increase the number of *true* beliefs we have— rather than live what we *know* is a lie.

Having discussed some preliminary matters, let's look now at seven important principles related to the unavoidability of truth. Perhaps we could call them: "Seven Principles for Highly Relativistic People"!

Principle #1:

RELATIVISM IS SELF-CONTRADICTORY

This means that because relativism claims to be *absolutely* true, it is false and should be rejected.

If a statement is self-contradictory, it simply can't be true. If I tell you, "I can't speak a word of English" or "No sentence is longer than six words" or "I don't exist," then you can conclude that what I have just said is false. It is quite apparent to you that I *can* speak English, that there *are* sentences longer than six words, and that I must *exist* in order to speak! Because I have contradicted myself in these sentences, my statements should be rejected. They are false.

Relativism is another example of a self-contradictory viewpoint; it should therefore be rejected as false. The relativist believes that *relativism is true*—not just for him but for everyone. We can ask the relativist: "Do you believe that relativism is true? If it's true, is it *absolutely* true for everyone, or is it just true for you?" Now if the relativist says that his view is true for *everyone*, then it is no longer relative but absolute. Thus the view is self-contradictory and therefore false.

But what if the relativist says, "This is just my view; it's just true for me, and you don't have to believe it?" Well, if *this* is the relativist's position, then what he is saying is on the same level of asserting, "Vanilla ice cream tastes better to you, but chocolate tastes better to me." So the relativist is saying *nothing* that is worthy of being believed by another; he is just giving his own opinion. But usually relativists believe they are giving more than their own opinion. In fact, the famous relativistic slogan— "That's true for *you*, but not for me"—presupposes that relativism applies to at least *two people*! The relativist believes that relativism is true for *both* parties, not just one.

Yes, relativists certainly give the impression that they believe their view is true for everyone. And not only that: they often try to *persuade* others to believe their perspective. In fact, they are often willing to give *objective* reasons—that is, reasons that are true, independent of anyone's viewpoint—for why relativism is true and absolutism is false. For example, relativists might say, "So many people believe different things; therefore relativism is the inescapable conclusion." But we can point out that *at the very least* (a) their *basis* for holding to relativism (i.e., that so many people disagree) is *true—not false*, and that (b) the relativist's conclusion about the inevitability of relativism is also true, not false. So in actuality, the relativist is an absolutist in relativist's clothing.

The word *proselytize* has become a dirty word in our society: "Isn't it arrogant to try to 'convert' others to your viewpoint? Don't you give the impression that you are right and others are wrong?" I once came across a newspaper article by a professor at Furman University who claimed that it was wrong for Christians to proselytize others. The irony of this essay is that this professor was attempting to do what he said Christians shouldn't do—namely, "convert" people to his own point of view. He was *proselytizing about not proselytizing*! This professor obviously thought that he was right and *not wrong*—*and* he wanted to let others know about it. Further, he thought he was somehow justified in trying to "convert" others to his viewpoint. But in his view, "dogmatic" Christians who evangelized were acting abominably. This is a typical inconsistency among relativists. They need to be reminded that if a relativist tries to convince people that relativism is true, he does not believe that it is just true for him, but true for *everyone*. After all, why try to persuade people about something that is no more than opinion—*unless* you believe it is really true and that others should believe it too?

Let me say something about the charge of *arrogance* here. When Christians tell others about the significance of Jesus Christ, they will not (if they are consistent) do so with a sense of superiority. The theologian Martin Luther said that telling another person about Jesus is *like one beggar's telling another beggar where to find bread.* Just as beggars can't be choosers, neither can they be braggarts! Since what Jesus offers is a gift, we can't take credit for it if we receive it. Belonging to God through Jesus is the result of God's kindness—not of earning it through our own efforts. When we find, say, a great cleaning product or an excellent restaurant, we tell others: "Check it out. It's terrific!" And the Christian says much the same thing: "Come and see" for yourself (John 1:46).

So we are not being arrogant *simply because* we believe that something is true. After all, people who disagree with those of us who hold to objective truth believe that we are *objectively wrong*! Does this mean *they* are being arrogant? You see, if we define "arrogance" as "the belief that one is right," then the relativist would have to be considered arrogant. Why? He believes that he is right and that those believing in absolutes are dead wrong. This is, of course, a double-standard ("I can say someone is wrong, but you can't!"). Arrogance, rather, deals primarily with an *attitude* rather than a *belief*, with *tone* rather than *truth-claim*.

Now let's get back to the unavoidability of truth. Presumably, the relativist believes that he has *good reasons* to hold to his position (e.g., "there are so many different points of view"). But if he offers some reason for why he believes that everything is relative and that no absolutes exist, *he believes his reasons are true and not false.* He believes his position is *justifiable and not arbitrary.* So no matter what position we happen to take, we will constantly be making truth-statements or presupposing certain truths to defend or justify our positions. And that's okay.

So let's lay to rest once and for all the question of whether objective truth exists or not. It is, as we have seen, *inescapable*. So since no one can escape it, we (even though we may disagree about *which* particular view is true) can advance the discussion to the next level—namely, the issue of *which* purportedly-true view best reflects or corresponds to objective reality and *why*.

REALITY IS OBJECTIVE

This means that no matter how much we think we shape reality, at some point we must admit that some of our very own beliefs (like the assumption that we can create *any* reality we want) are themselves *immune* to human manipulation. And no matter how strong the influence of genetics or environment upon us may be, we still possess at least *some* objectivity in order to draw conclusions about the strength of these influences.

∘━✦━∘

In September 1998, I wrote a letter to the editor of *The Wheel*, the student newspaper at Emory University in Atlanta. A student had written an essay on his assessment of the nature of reality. He claimed that reality is like a piece of wet clay—we can mold it any way we want to. So "my reality" can be completely different—and just as legitimate—as "your reality." But in this same article, he contradicted himself by making the very *opposite* point—namely, that reality is shaped by powerful forces beyond our control. He asserted that anyone who has seen *The Truman Show* or any student of sociology knows that social forces determine the "reality" in which we find ourselves.

Not surprisingly, the two opposing points offered by this student are very popular slogans in our day: (#1) *we all can shape reality any way we choose* and (#2) *reality is shaped for us by factors independent of us* (e.g., genetics, history, culture, language). Even though *both* cannot be true, let's examine each of them.

But first—what is *reality*? Is cyberspace "real"? Do newspapers report what is "real"? Although we'll indirectly address these sorts of issues below, let's assume as a working definition that what is *real* is that which *is*, that which *exists*. (So a unicorn is *not* real since it does not exist. On the other hand mathematical propositions such as 7+8=15 are *real* and thus exist— even though they are not physical objects. Such propositions would exist or be the case even if human minds *never* existed.) And if something is *true*, it will correspond to what *is*, to what *exists*.

Claim #1: "We shape our own reality": "That's just *your* reality," we're told. How do we respond to this frequently-heard slogan? Let's ask the person who says that each of us can shape his own reality if he *really* believes this. If he says yes, we can tell him: "Then you believe that there is at least one thing that cannot be shaped by human beings—that is, *the incontestable reality that everyone can shape his own reality.*" Or we can ask him: "Is your idea—that each of us can shape his own reality—nothing more than some reality that *you* have created? If so, *why do you think it applies to me at all?*" Of course, our friend certainly appears to be saying that his view *does* apply to everyone. In that case, he has contradicted himself. He ultimately believes that not *all* reality can be created. Some things are real or exist, about which we can do absolutely nothing.

There is, thus, at least *some* objective reality that applies to everyone. So we're not being "arrogant" or "imperialistic" if we assert that *some* aspect of reality cannot be manipulated by human thought or action. If a person strongly disagrees with us, he will presumably do so on the basis of a reality he thinks *applies to both parties*! So even if a person is incorrect about what actually *is* real, everyone inescapably believes that some kind of objective reality exists. So, again, the discussion can move beyond the question, "Does objective reality exist?" to "Given that objective reality exists and is unavoidable, how do I *justify or support* my particular views regarding objective reality?"

Perhaps it's worth mentioning one commonly-held belief: "Truth is *what you sincerely believe.*" Sincerity, according to this statement, *makes* something true—a kind of reality-creation. For example, if I sincerely believe that Marxism or some form of Eastern philosophy is true, then it somehow *becomes* true. But I can think of a lot of things that are *false* or *wrong* no matter how sincerely one might believe that they are "true" or "good"—sincere serial-killing, sincere rape, sincere torture, sincere random-shootings, sincere Fascism, sincere Satanism. Sincerity does not make 2+2=5, nor does it alter the law of gravity. Simply by sincerely believing, I can't bring my lost loved one back from the dead. Sincerity won't change the fact that my favorite baseball team, the Cleveland Indians, lost the World Series to the Atlanta Braves in 1995 and then to the Florida Marlins in 1997.

You may have seen the bumper sticker: "God said it! I believe it! That settles it!" But let's ask ourselves: "If God exists and communicates with human beings, then how does my believing it (or not) settle anything at all?" A more accurate rendering of this slogan would be: "God said it! That settles it *whether I believe it or not*!" So we have to differentiate between the *truth* of a particular belief (for example, 2+2=4) and the *belief* itself (for example, I may *not* believe that 2+2=4). How does my sincerely believing something *make* it true? Had it been *false* before and then it *became* true? Why not, instead, accept the common-sense intuition we share and live by each day—that things are true or false *whether we believe them or not*? After all, sincerely believing won't make rush hour traffic or mounting utility bills go away!

Furthermore, this "sincere-belief" criterion for truth is itself a *fixed* and *absolute* rule by those who proclaim it. In essence, they say, "You are *wrong* and *mistaken* if you disagree with my view that sincere belief makes something true." So the person who believes that reality is *not* created by sincerity can reply: "What if I *sincerely believe* that that believing something sincerely *does not* make something true?" This question reveals the self-contradictory nature of the notion that truth is created by sincere belief; this would mean that *both* of these "sincere" believers would be correct—but holding to contradictory points of view. The "sincere-belief" person believes that his criterion is true, and that those who disagree with him are *wrong*.

Someone might object by saying: "Don't we at least create reality through certain choices we make? Don't I create a certain reality by renting one video rather than another or by choosing one particular flavor of Ben and Jerry's ice cream rather than another?" Of course, our present choices *do* make a difference and give shape to certain realities. But the crucial point is this: *once we have made the choice, it is an unalterable reality that the choice cannot be un-chosen.* That is, it is metaphysically (or in reality) impossible to change the past—whether by humans or by God. (Remember that God's power does not extend to the self-contradictory or nonsensical, such as making square circles or making a stone so big that he can't lift it. *No* power can bring about these states of affairs. Similarly, this pertains to "unfixing" the necessarily fixed past as well.) The past has a certain "hardness" to it that the future does not. No amount of human manipulation can alter what has already taken place—though we may try to *deny* or *suppress* the past. Therefore, *the past is a reality we have to acknowledge*; it is not a wet lump of clay to mold any way we want.

So we see that *all* reality can't be shaped by our choosing or by our sincerely believing, and we must come to grips with this fact.

Claim #2: "Reality is shaped by forces beyond our control": This second view is a kind of determinism. That is, whatever we happen to think or do or say can ultimately be traced to a preceding series of causes and effects. The present has been determined by the past. The conclusion people draw from such an assumption is this: No matter how hard we try to gain objectivity or arrive at the truth about a matter, our historical and cultural context or our genetic make-up ultimately overpowers us. Thus, all we can say is, "This is just *my* perspective"—and no more.

Earlier I made passing mention of *The Truman Show*. This movie is about a man named Truman Burbank (Jim Carrey). His life is literally a TV show in a sheltered environment called "Seahaven." Everyone in his life is an actor or actress. This "world within a world" is equipped with 5,000 cameras, which monitor Truman's every move. He thinks that *this* is reality. In the movie, Christof (Ed Harris) is the producer of the *Truman Show* and the manipulator of Truman's life. He says: "While the world [Truman] inhabits is somewhat counterfeit, Truman is genuine." Marlon, an artificial "friend" of Truman's, says about the show: "It's all true. It's all real. Nothing here is fake. . . . It's merely controlled." Despite the fact that Truman eventually flees from his artificial world to discover the *real* world, the movie raises interesting questions about reality.

In the scenario we're presently considering, it is claimed that we actually don't have *any* power to create our own reality. Rather, it has been determined for us by forces beyond our control.

Before looking into this second claim, we should recognize the humbling truth about ourselves: We are limited and never as objective as we'd like to be. Our cultural environment, family background, place in history, and a host of other factors can and often do distort our perceptions. We aren't 100% bias-free, purely-objective individuals. That's the downside. On more of a positive note, we can *still* achieve objectivity despite an array of influences that shape us. To deny the possibility of *any* truth statements or *any* objectivity is to declare this as a *true* and *objective* fact: "it's *objectively true* that we can't know something as objectively true!"

It's interesting that those who say that we

have been determined by these social or genetic forces *don't really* believe that they themselves have been. When someone says, "We're just the products of our environment or our genes," he doesn't believe this statement is nothing more than the product of his environment or his genes. Rather, he believes that there is *good reason* to hold such a view, that his view has been *reflected upon* and *rationally justified*; so he makes himself an exception to his own rule. Furthermore, if this determinist really believed his own statement, then he would have to affirm another contradiction: He would have to say that *both* (a) *his* views on anything *and* (b) *all opposing views* would be on the same level since both are the products of culture or genes or whatever. If our environment or culture or genetic make-up is responsible for what we think and do, then there is no rational way to tell *which* view (if any) is true. Take the geneticist and Nobel Prize winner, Francis Crick. He writes in his book, *The Astonishing Hypothesis*:

> The Astonishing Hypothesis is that "You," your joys and your sorrows, your memories and your ambitions, your sense of personal identity and free will, are in fact no more than the behavior of a vast assembly of nerve cells and their associated molecules. . . . This hypothesis is so alien to the ideas of most people today that it can truly be called "astonishing."

On the contrary, what is *truly* astonishing is what Crick *fails* to see: if Crick is right, then his book is "no more than the behavior of a vast assembly of nerve cells and their associated molecules"! Crick gives the impression that he, unlike the rest of us, has somehow been able to evade the physiological forces that determine what the rest of us think. (This has been called the "self-excepting fallacy.") He gives the impression that *his* particular nerve cells and their associated molecules had absolutely *nothing* to do with his conclusions!

In a similar vein, the behaviorist makes a similar claim—that human beings are nothing more than the product of their personal background; freedom is an illusion, and our choices are simply the predictable outcome of a series of pre-existing conditions. In a September 1983 issue of *Psychology Today*, the famous behaviorist and author of *Walden Two*, B.F. Skinner, declared: "If I am right about human behavior, I have written the autobiography of a nonperson . . . . So far as I know, my behavior at any given moment has been nothing more than the product of my genetic endowment, my personal history, and the current setting." But again, Skinner's very statement should not be taken as asserting anything objectively true. Rather, what he said was itself "nothing more than the product of [his] genetic endowment, [his] personal history, and the current setting." Thus there's no good reason to *believe* what he claimed. If Skinner were correct, then it was purely by accident, not by his rationally concluding this.

The study of history bears out another illuminating example. Keith Windschuttle, an Australian historian, has documented the decline of serious historical study in our day. His book *The Killing of History* indicates that historians are increasingly less inclined to believe that there is any distinction between myth and fact, between fiction and non-fiction. The writing of history is virtually no different from propaganda. Or it can be seen as the attempt of one racial, social, or political grouping to assert power over another.

This leads us to ask: And what of *these very historians* who claim that writing history is nothing more than asserting power or nothing more than a reflection of ever-changing cultural ideas? What should we make of the claim that we cannot distinguish between fiction and non-fiction? As you probably notice, such assertions end up either being mired in self-*contradiction*—or they *say nothing* at all. On the one hand, the "expert" who maintains that we can't distinguish between fiction and non-fiction in history doesn't *really* believe this. After all, he believes that at least his statement is *not fictitious*! When he is speaking or writing, he presumably expects that his audience will take him to be saying something factual rather than mythical! He certainly doesn't want them to be wondering: "Is this scholar giving me fact or fiction?" Thus the relativistic historian *contradicts himself* by making his own views the exception to the rule. On the other hand, if all history-writing is an assertion of power or the product of one's social environment, then the person making this claim is doing nothing more than exerting power or expressing what his social environment has dictated for him to believe. In other words, *he says nothing meaningful.* His view is no different than the next person's, both of whom have been completely shaped by external factors.

Before completing this segment, it might be beneficial to note other slogans that fit into this category. Let's try this one: *"There are no facts—only interpretations."* This is commonly asserted, but let's ask the question we've been raising in this section: Does the person asserting this statement make himself an *exception* to this statement? Clearly, the person who says that there are no facts—only interpretations—believes that this statement is *factual*, not merely *interpretive*!

Here's another: *"There is no reality—only appearances."* (As Woody Allen once mused: "What if everything is an illusion and nothing exists? In that case I definitely overpaid for my carpet.") However, the person who declares this believes that *at least this statement properly reflects reality*! And, furthermore, if there is no reality, aren't the *appearances themselves* real?

A final slogan to note is this one—*"Question authority!"* Although there is undoubtedly a tendency for, say, political authorities to overstep their bounds, there is something fundamentally flawed in the assumption of this quip. This slogan *presupposes an authority of its own*, doesn't it? It essentially says this: "Question all authority, but don't question *my* authority!" Some kind of objective (or, dare we say, *authoritative*) standpoint will be inevitable; objectivity is inescapable. Those who deny it will make themselves exceptions to their own rule.

Again, those who reduce all that we think and do to genetics, environment, reproduction and survival, or language do one of two things: (a) they *contradict themselves* by acting as though they have escaped the influences everyone else is subject to (the self-excepting fallacy); or (b) they *say nothing at all* since what they express is nothing more than the product of those influences.

LOGIC IS NOT ARBITRARY

This means that if we deny the validity of logic, we will end up *using* logic in order to do so.

⚬━━⚬

Logical thinking has fallen on hard times. In Neil Postman's critique of media culture, *Amusing Ourselves To Death*, he reveals how Americans of previous generations were far more capable of serious thought than we are today with our 15-second sound-bites, commercials, and 30-minute shows which raise and solve extremely complex and difficult problems. Literate Americans in the past were far more articulate and literarily skilled than they are today. According to Benjamin Franklin, Americans in his day were committed to the printed word. Every village had a lecture hall, and factory workers and artisans, men and women, would regularly go hear lectures. When Abraham Lincoln debated Stephen Douglas in Ottowa, Illinois in 1858, the format of the debate was as follows: Douglas would speak for 60 minutes; Lincoln would respond for 90 minutes; then Douglas would have 30 minutes for a rebuttal. In an earlier debate in Peoria (1854), Douglas delivered a three-hour address, and then Lincoln (after a break) responded for four more hours. That's seven hours of talk in one day—complete with complex sentences and lengthy argument!

By contrast, today's public debates tend to be reduced to brief slogans. Typical mailings from an array of political-action or social organizations allow no room for reasoned, nuanced discussion of the issues. Complex arguments are "dumbed down"; the opposing side is demonized; and still-deeper polarization of the issues is generated. Our visual culture—with billboards, TVs, and videos—presents a message that does not make the demands that the printed page does. Reading is an *activity* which requires processing and sequential thinking whereas watching tends to be *passive* and does not necessitate thoughtful analysis. The fallout from this cultural decline is the serious neglect of reason. For instance, when we present our case to someone, we are disappointed to hear that conversation-stopper, "Whatever!"

Many people think that logic is irrelevant. "That's just *your* logic," they'll say. But to reject logical objectivity is self-contradictory. How so? We will end up *using* logic by *denying* its validity. Let me illustrate what I mean. Alan Watts was an Anglican clergyman who later became a Buddhist. After long attempts to reconcile Christianity and Buddhism, he decided that Christianity was "incorrigibly theistic" and "invincibly self-righteous" and couldn't be harmonized with his Eastern philosophical beliefs. To justify his rejection of Christianity in favor of Buddhism, Watts proposed that logic could not "bind" or govern reality. True knowledge, which can't be explained or described, is ultimately nonrational.

Watts dismissed the rationality of Christianity—with its making truth-claims about doctrine and particular historical events—

as expressing useless "Western logic." But here's the serious problem: To reject Christianity, *Watts used the very logic he denied as valid.* He knew that Christianity and Buddhism were—though he didn't use the word—*logically* incompatible, and he assumed that he had an objective measuring rod by which he came to judge Christianity as being wrong. Yet as he *chose* "Eastern logic" (the absorbent *both/and* kind) rather than "Western logic" (the either/or kind), he had to use the "either/or" method in his selection. Put simply, he had to *use* "Western" (or Aristotelian) logic in order to reject "Western" logic! "Western" logic is *inescapable* because it is bound up with the way things are. So, like it or not, laws of logic are fundamental to how we live and think and are part of the world around us.

The notion that something is "true for you but not for me" is often applied in a broader context to argue that no system of logic—whether Aristotle's or some subsequently formulated system—is superior to another. So one may claim, "*Your* logic may suit you, but there are other systems of logic around. So don't think that *mine* is illegitimate." But each of these logical systems *presupposes* fundamental laws discovered by Aristotle; they are not simply applicable within Aristotle's system and nowhere else! Furthermore, logical laws, even simple everyday conversation would be impossible. As I point out below, logical laws apply to the particular words we use in sentences and to drawing everyday conclusions about *why* a car isn't working or *why* a power outage occurred.

What are some of these basic logical laws? Let me mention two. There is the *law of non-*

contradiction ("A is not non-A"). This states that if something is self-contradictory—such as relativism—it can't be true. For example, if I say that "Socrates existed" and then say "Socrates never existed," I am contradicting myself; what I have said is therefore false because it is contrary to a fundamental logical law. Or say I am wearing a blue tie. The law of non-contradiction says that the tie cannot be both blue and non-blue (e.g., green) at the same time and in the same respect. Now the tie could be dyed to a green color tomorrow, but it couldn't be green and blue tomorrow *at the same instant.* So while the same tie could be dyed a different color, at the *present* moment it is blue, not green.

There is also the *law of excluded middle* ("either something is A or non-A"). Whereas the law of non-contradiction maintains that no statement can be both true and false, this law declares that any proposition is either true or false. This law states that there exist *only* two (or three or whatever number) alternatives regarding the truth-status of a certain claim, and if one alternative is false, then it must be the other (or one of the others) that is true. There is no middle ground (*tertium quid*). For example, either God exists or he doesn't. I can't say, "God exists, but only in my mind." If God exists *only* in my mind, then God—traditionally understood as the all-good, self-existing, personal Creator and Sustainer of life—does not exist. There is no middle ground on the matter. Now Watt's rejection of Christianity was a living demonstration of how this law works. He knew that there was no compromise of or synthesis between the two religious alternatives with which he began— Christianity and Buddhism. He just could not blend the two. It was one or the other. So he rejected the Christian faith.

When people say, "That's just your logic," they are utilizing the law of non-contradiction. They are admitting to the truth that these two "logics" are not the identical. Even when people say to you, "Whatever!" or just keep silent, they are implicitly admitting that their viewpoint is *logically distinct* from yours.

Someone might protest, "But doesn't language *condition* our logic? Isn't logic nothing more than the product of how we use language?" The underlying assumption here is that language shapes our very thinking, and we can't have any access to the "real world" outside our minds—including the very logic we use. But let's ask ourselves: Which is *more basic or fundamental*—language or logic? That is, which is really necessary for which? Again, it seems inescapable that logical laws are necessary for language and not the other way around. To illustrate, let's take a simple sentence—"The cat sat on the mat." Even this sentence presupposes a certain underlying logic which is necessary for the sentence's intelligibility. When we say "cat," we mean something quite distinct from "mat." When we say "sat," we do not mean "ran" or "ate." So even at the level of word usage, we *already* presuppose basic logical distinctions. That is, logic is necessary for language even to get off the ground.

MAKING JUDGMENTS IS INEVITABLE

This means that if we think one should never "judge," but then point out that *others* are "judging," we ourselves have just *made a judgment.*

⚜

A lot of people who don't usually read the Bible are often fond of quoting a particular Bible verse—Matthew 7:1: "Do not judge lest you also be judged." These people somehow get the idea that Jesus was saying, "Never say anyone is in error or call someone's actions wrong."

This, however, is an example of highly selective quoting. These people who so readily cite Matthew 7:1 probably haven't even heard of the verse from John 7:24. There Jesus says, "Don't judge by mere appearances, but make a *right* judgment." What's this? We're to make judgments? Yes, but not superficial ones.

What then does Jesus mean in Matthew 7:1? Certainly Jesus does *not* mean that judging is saying some act or belief is wrong. If that were the case, those who quote this verse to you would be *judging you for judging others*! What Jesus was talking about was not a kind of judging that never discerns between right or wrong, good or evil. Rather, Jesus is saying that we shouldn't think that we are better than another person because we haven't done the wrong that the other person has. We can feel pretty good about ourselves when others fall on their face. We can be smug when we haven't done that particular wrong. This type of attitude we could call *judgmentalism*—as opposed to simply making a judgment between right and wrong. Jesus warns us to be careful, to remember that we too could do the very same thing. Jesus essentially says, "Check yourself *first* so that you're not proud or you don't think you're above temptation [take the plank out of your own eye]. *Then* you can help the person who needs help [then you can take the speck out of the other's eye]."

So judging—which we can distinguish from being *judgmental*—at *some* level will be inevitable. And that is all right too. We just have to keep in mind that we all have feet of clay ("there, but for the grace of God, go I"). With this mindset, we can help people who are in the wrong—*just as* we hope people will help *us* when *we* are in the wrong.

TOLERANCE MUST BE CLARIFIED

That is, the tolerance which "accepts" all views as true or legitimate will be self-contradictory. But *true* tolerance recognizes the difference between *persons*, who should be treated with respect, and their *beliefs*, with which we need not agree.

Relativism has its ironies. Despite the fact that it proclaims a freedom from absolute truth, relativists still hold to the absolute of tolerance. If there is *anything* that is morally wrong today, it is intolerance! Again, we have another contradiction within relativism—besides the *absolute denial* of absolutes, we have the *absolute wrongness* of intolerance! Before we go further, though, we must take note of what true tolerance is.

If you're told, "You're being intolerant," the first order of business is to find out *how* tolerance is being defined or understood. A lot of people think that if you believe you are right and someone else is wrong, then you are being intolerant. But this is a misunderstanding. Historically, tolerance has been defined as "putting up with beliefs one takes to be erroneous or false." In fact, we often use "tolerance" in this way today. Most people tolerate Brussels sprouts or liver when served it as guests, but no one tolerates what he enjoys (chocolate or ice cream). Today, though, some people have said that tolerance means "*accepting* all views as true and not saying any are false." But if we define tolerance this way, then we'll start accepting views that contradict one another. The relativist will be put in the awkward spot of believing *his* view—that everything is relative—and *my* view—that *absolutes* exist. But the relativist *by definition* cannot accept an absolutist's view as true.

But there is a way out. One can be tolerant in a *consistent* manner. Tolerance, *properly* understood, means that we respect people enough to permit them to hold their beliefs even if we profoundly disagree with them. Tolerance says that *all people should be accepted as possessing dignity and thus as being worthy of respect.* This does not mean we have to accept their views as true or that they are worthy of belief. True tolerance distinguishes between *people* and *beliefs*; genuine tolerance is the acceptance and respectful treatment of other people—*even if* we don't accept their views. Remember that the relativist will *never* accept the absolutist's view as true or legitimate. And you've probably noticed how some people can say that we should accept all views as true—*until* they talk to someone who doesn't accept all views as true! At this point, all logic often stops, and insulting begins!

One final word on tolerance: We must strike a balance between conviction of the truth and graciousness or civility in manner. Some people, having strong convictions about their beliefs, can often lack civility in their demeanor. Yet others are so "nice" that they have no boldness and no conviction regarding standards of truth and morality. They are too cowardly to stand up for anything. The proper approach lies in the middle: both *heartlessness* and *spinelessness* must be replaced by speaking the *truth* in *love* (Ephesians 4:10).

MORAL RELATIVISM IS UNLIVABLE

This means that people *really* do think it is wrong to violate their rights, and even relativists get *upset* and *offended* at the apparent "immorality" of moral absolutes.

"Who are *you* to impose your morality on others?" "How can you say another culture's moral standards are inferior?" People who parrot these slogans reject "moralizers" who speak as though they have the ethical high ground. To say that some action is wrong is to pontificate when one has no business doing so.

I once read a "letter to the editor," in which the writer claimed that morality was "personal" and "subjective." The writer said that he was angered and deeply offended when people—especially "religious" sorts—sought to "impose" *their* standards of morality on everyone else. It all sounded so arrogant.

Again, I offered a response to this letter. I pointed out that this relativist actually *did* hold to certain objective moral standards. For example, he believed that it was *morally wrong* to say that someone else is wrong! One *ought not* pontificate about moral values. I pointed out that he *wanted to impose his morality on those who wanted to impose their morality on others*!

Furthermore, I said that I could not figure out why a relativist would be *offended* or *angered* by those who believed in moral absolutes. Why get so uptight if everything is relative? My point was that this letter was *saturated* with absolute moral standards—but all in the name of an apparently "tolerant" relativism.

This leads us to discuss what has been called the "anthropologist's mistake," which assumes that there is no moral law "above" the cultures of the world—a view typically held by cultural anthropologists. Rather, each culture has its own moral system, and it is arrogant and imperialistic to claim that morality in the West is "superior" to other cultures. We should just "leave them alone," we're told. The "anthropologist's view," however, is problematic and mistaken.

First, the "anthropologist's view" is *itself* a moral position: it asserts that it is *morally wrong* to claim moral superiority over another culture. (The cultural anthropologist's charges of being "arrogant," "imperialistic," "bigoted," and "intolerant" deal with *universally valid moral* standards. The anthropologist believes that no one *ought* to act in this manner.)

Second, this view denies the intuitively obvious—that there are objective moral facts. Let's look at some examples. *Tsujigir*—a "crossroads cut"—was an ancient practice of Samurai warriors in Japan; the Samurai would test his new sword by cutting a person in two. Another example is *suttee*: Before being outlawed in India by the British, this practice of burning a widow alive on the funeral pyre of her dead husband was common. A frequently-used example is the Third Reich of the Nazis, who murdered 6 million Jews, almost completely eradicated the gypsies of Europe, and brought untold suffering and death upon millions more. Stalin had some 20 million put to death through his "purges" (my own grandfather died of starvation in one of Stalin's labor camps). Clearly, there *are* undeniable moral norms such as "torturing babies for fun is wrong"; "murder or theft is wrong"; "kindness is good."

Third, the anthropologist wrongly assumes "Western arrogance" when we criticize the apparently "immoral" practices of other cultures. But this is not so. While it is the case that cultures practicing cannibalism or infanticide are simply *defective* in their morality, this does not mean that the Westerner cannot criticize the greed or political corruption within his *own* culture. Each culture has its own virtues to be embraced as well as vices to be rejected.

Fourth, the anthropologist's mistake prohibits any sort of moral reform from taking place. If the anthropologist had has way, there would have been no abolition of the slave trade, no women's suffrage, no Civil Rights movement, no banning of apartheid in South Africa. What makes the idea of moral *reform* coherent is some objective moral ideal toward which we can strive.

Moral relativism is intuitively implausible. And when we are willing to ask *serious* questions about morality, we find that we don't *really* believe that moral values are relative. Just ask yourself: "Do you *right now* believe that it's okay to murder or to be murdered?" You might think: "Well, some people have thought so." But the question is: "Do you—not other people—*right now* have any doubt about the wrongness of murder?" *This* is the place to begin—not what other people have alleged. So we don't have to waste our time talking about what we both accept as true. We can, instead, begin discussing the real issue—namely, which viewpoint *best accounts* for the existence of objective moral values.

But not only is moral relativism rationally problematic. It is also *practically unlivable*. That is, we human beings—even if we are *blind* to certain moral defects within us or our culture, can *still recognize* the violation of certain human rights and basic moral standards when they confront us.

The Christian philosopher J.P. Moreland has written about an illuminating encounter with a student at the University of Vermont. J.P. was speaking in a dorm, and a relativistic student who lived there told him, "Whatever is true for you is true for you and whatever is true for me is true for me. If something works for you because you believe it, that's great. But no one should force his or her views on other people since everything is relative." J.P. told him that his view implied that there was no such thing as sin or wrongdoing, and the student readily agreed. Then as J.P. left, he unplugged the student's stereo and started out the door with it.

The student protested: "Hey, what are you doing? . . . . You can't do that!"

J.P. replied, "You're not going to *force* on me the belief that it is wrong to steal your stereo, are you?" He then went on to point out to the student that when it's convenient, people will say they don't care about sexual morality or cheating on exams. But they become moral absolutists in a hurry when someone steals *their* things or violates *their* rights. That is, they are *selective* moral relativists. It's okay for anyone to do anything—*until* it disrupts *my* life or violates *my* rights.

Then it's time to become a moral absolutist!

Robert Wengert, a philosophy professor at the University of Illinois, would ask his ethics class if his students thought truth was relative. The majority of students typically raised their hands. Then Wengert would tell them that short students would get A's while tall students would fail. When his students would protest that his grading system wasn't fair and that he *ought* not or *should* not grade in that fashion, Wengert pointed out to his class that when they used words like *ought* or *should*, they revealed a belief in an objective moral standard. They really didn't believe that morality is relative.

There are other practical problems with moral relativism. *First*, we can never make moral progress if everything is relative. Why exert moral effort to become a better, more virtuous person if morality isn't objective? Why even bother with "random acts of kindness" when kindness isn't objectively different from cruelty? *Second*, if morality is relative, then one choice is as legitimate as another—to rape or to save from rape, to murder or to protect from murder. Do we *really* want to grant relativism intellectual legitimacy in the face of such problems?

Although I cannot fully take up the theme of alternative views of morality here,[2] let me say something briefly about offering some kind of basis for the existence of objective morality. If God existed, we would certainly *expect* objective moral values to exist. Such values would not be surprising or unnatural at all. After all, if we humans have been made to resemble God in certain important respects, if we have been created in "the image" of a personal, good God (as traditional theism affirms), then we should not wonder that each of us has intrinsic dignity and worth, that we are morally responsible agents, that we have the capacity to recognize moral truths, and that we have certain moral obligations. It should, further, be noted that morality relates only to *persons*—not to rocks or nonpersonal entities like ants, rats, or chimps, which are not morally responsible and have no moral obligations.

But if God does not exist, then we can rightly ask: "How does objective morality emerge from non-moral processes? If God does not exist, *on what basis* should I think that I have intrinsic dignity and worth? How does one account for this emergence of dignity if nature is all there is? If there are moral laws to the universe, then why think that they have to do only with us humans and not other living organisms?"

Of course, people can be atheists or non-theists (i.e., who do not believe in a personal God) and *still* share the same moral values as theists (who believe in a personal God). Furthermore, they can develop moral systems which assert the same kinds of values that the theist affirms. This is not surprising since atheists too have been made in the image of a good God—even though they do not acknowledge this. So the issue to face is not, "Do *I recognize* certain moral values to be objectively true?" Rather, it is, "If I recognize these moral values to be true, which viewpoint offers the *best foundation* for these moral values? Is it a viewpoint which presupposes an impersonal, non-moral, unguided series of steps in a long naturalistic process? Or is it a viewpoint which presupposes a personal, good Creator and Designer, who has made us to relate personally to him and to live our lives according to the pattern which reflects his moral character (theism)? It seems clear that theism, which is *super*naturalistic (there is a reality *beyond* nature), offers a more plausible picture for affirming these values than does a naturalistic one.

So we have seen that moral relativism is rationally indefensible and practically unlivable. Furthermore, if we do affirm objective moral values and intrinsic human dignity, a theistic context helps us make better sense of these moral facts than does an atheistic or non-theistic one.

Principle #3:

RELIGIOUS PLURALISM IS EXCLUSIVISTIC

This means that if someone believes all religions lead to salvation or liberation, he believes he has a virtue that persons within a particular religious tradition do not have: that is, he believes he has the correct perspective —the "God's eye-view"—and traditional religious adherents do not. And this was the very problem he was opposing at the outset!

⚬━━⚬

In a radio interview, a woman related to me the words of her mother: "You can't come to any conclusions about religion or politics." I pointed out that her mother had in fact *come to a conclusion* about religion and politics—namely, that no conclusion could be drawn about them! This is the sort of problem that emerges with religious pluralists, who are on the increase in light of the global village in which we find ourselves.

What is religious pluralism? It claims that *all* religions lead to salvation or liberation— whether Christianity, Hinduism, Islam, or Buddhism. All religions are *culturally-conditioned attempts* to move from self-centeredness to Reality-centeredness—whether we call this Reality *Allah, Jehovah, Krishna,* or *Brahman.* So the pluralist believes the idea that only one religious tradition can offer the sole path of salvation is intolerant and imperialistic.

As I have offered criticisms of religious pluralism in my book "*True for You, But Not for Me*," I'll only make some very general comments here. As we'll see shortly, the pluralist falls prey to the same sorts of criticisms that the relativist does. As with truth, reality, and morality, making objective truth-claims about religion is also inescapable.

Now the pluralist tends to believe it is arrogant to say that one's religious worldview is true; he often sees the traditional religious person as assuming that "all other religions are completely false." But the traditional Christian, say, affirms that the Christian faith is true, and where others disagree with it, they are in error *at that point*. The important phrase is "at that point." For it would be *naïve* and *wrong* to make the sweeping statement: "All other religions are *completely* false." Certainly, much truth can be found within differing religious traditions. As Jewish theologian Moses Maimonides said, "Accept the truth, whatever its source." So the Christian, who believes that all truth is God's truth, can affirm that there are many other truths within other religious belief-systems. The point of contention is where they *disagree*. If the Christian is correct in believing, for instance, that Jesus of Nazareth died on a Roman cross, then the Muslim, who denies this, would be in error—and vice versa.

At any rate, the pluralist thinks that the Christian viewpoint is in error because Christians are taking a "God's eye-view" on religious matters. Yet the pluralist himself believes that his pluralistic views are correct, non-arbitrary, and worthy of universal assent while the views of traditional religionists are cul-

turally-conditioned, arbitrary, and not universally binding! Our point here is that *some*
"God's eye-view" on religion will be unavoidable. (Whether the pluralist or the religionist
view is right or wrong is another matter!) Again,
we see that it's perfectly fine to hold to religious
truths; after all, we can't escape them.

You have probably heard of the parable of
six blind men before the king of Benares, India.
Each is touching one part of the elephant, and
each tries to describe the elephant from his limited vantage point: "It's a pillar"; "It's a rope";
etc. While this image appears to illustrate what
many in our society think about religion, certain
ironies and even contradictions begin to emerge
within the religious pluralist's system.

In the first place, *if religious beliefs are simply
culturally-conditioned responses to the Ultimate
Reality, then religious pluralism is another one of
those culturally-conditioned responses*! Yet the religious pluralist gives the impression that his own
view is not culturally conditioned; instead, it is an
objective assessment of the status of all religions.
The point here is *not* whether we should make
assessments about religions since such assessments are unavoidable. (Just think about it: To
say, "You can't come to any firm conclusions
about religions," is to draw a firm conclusion
about religion). Rather, the point is that the
pluralist's claim is far less modest than he alleges.

Second, *the religious pluralist cannot escape
an exclusivistic point of view.* What do we mean
by exclusivism? Although this idea of exclusivism can be understood in a couple of different senses (which I'll mention below), the sense
to which I'm referring here has to do with being
able to make objective pronouncements about

the truth or falsity of religious beliefs, having a kind of "God's eye-view" about them. As I noted earlier, this type of exclusivism is unavoidable. The religious pluralist is *also* subject to the same kind of criticism as the traditional Christian or Muslim. Despite the pluralist's attempt to appear more "tolerant" than adherents of a particular religious tradition, we find that pluralism is *still* exclusivistic. That is, the pluralist believes that he has a virtue that the Christian, the Muslim, or the Buddhist does not have. He believes that he is right, and that others are wrong where they disagree with him!

In doing so, the pluralist commits the error that he believes the religious exclusivist to be committing: He believes he is right, and any beliefs which disagree with his own are therefore false—but this is exclusivistic. So *who* in the parable of the six blind men represents the pluralist? It is *the king* who is looking on! The pluralist doesn't believe that *he* is one of the blind men, who is giving his own partial and flawed perspective on religion. He believes that he clearly sees what the blind men do not! It is hard to understand, then, how the pluralist can escape the charge of "narrowness" or "exclusivity" that he levels at the exclusivist.

Now the pluralist may respond by saying: "The kind of 'exclusivism' I am opposing is not one which rejects the possibility of truth and error within religions; after all, truth and error are unavoidable. However, when one claims that *one particular religion*—like the Christian faith—is the only means of salvation, I think this is arrogant and imperialistic since those outside of it must inevitably be excluded from salvation, from experiencing the joy of God's presence forever." This view of exclusivism, however, is a misunderstanding and requires clarification. (I deal with this question extensively in my book *"True for You, But Not for Me."*) To the contrary, the Christian faith maintains that *everyone* is invited to share in salvation and forgiveness from the guilt of moral wrongdoing or sin; *no one* is excluded from this invitation. (So "exclusivism" can be a misleading term.) As 2 Peter 3:9 indicates, God isn't willing that anyone be excluded from salvation; he desires that all people come into a right relationship with him rather than be separated from him. Surely he is great enough to make this reconciliation possible for all people. Although this issue requires further clarification and nuanced discussion, I have argued in my book that salvation through Christ is *potentially accessible to all*—even if they have not heard of him, even if they are "unevangelized." The joy of knowing God and of experiencing his presence forever is available to all. It is *human beings* who resist God's loving initiative and are thus justly separated from God forever. They get what they want—*no God*. In the end, the relevant question to ask regarding those who have never heard would be: *If* the unevangelized *were* to hear and understand the Christian message of forgiveness through Jesus of Nazareth, *would* they respond?

Third, *all religions are exclusivistic*: Many today wrongly believe that Christianity is the only religion that is exclusivistic. (Here is use "exclusivism" in both of the senses mentioned above.) However, as I briefly noted earlier, not only is the pluralist taking an exclusivistic stance when he maintains that there are true and false beliefs within religion. People within *all* religions are exclusivistic; that is, they take their beliefs to be true and not false, and (in many cases) rejecting them jeopardizes one's salvation or liberation. For example, Gautama Buddha, who grew up in a Hindu environment, ended up rejecting (1) the Vedic scriptures of Hinduism and (2) the Hindu doctrine of the enduring soul. Muhammad, the founder of Islam, rejected the polytheism (belief in many gods) of his day in favor of monotheism (belief in one God). Furthermore, the Buddhist will reject the traditional Christian doctrine of the enduring soul and the belief in a future bodily resurrection. And whereas the Christian believes that desire, when it is properly focused (e.g., desiring or yearning after God), is good, the Buddhist believes that all desire is the source of suffering. Unfortunately, many perceive Christianity to be "dogmatic" and "rigid," and they resort to "Christian-bashing" in one form or another. But the truth is that all religions have a dogma or set of doctrinal truths to be embraced, and in most cases the rejection of these tenets results in a forfeiture (or, at best, postponement) of salvation.

Fourth, *rationality of belief is more important than the geography of belief:* The religious pluralist will say, "If you were born in India, you would most likely have been a Hindu. If you were born in Saudi Arabia, you probably would have become a Muslim." While statistically this is true, religious pluralism is not at all proved by this point. Let me make two points to bear this out.

Point # 1: We could reply: "If someone grows up in a *pluralistic* society, he'll likely be a *pluralist.* But what conclusion should we draw from this fact? Should he no longer be a pluralist?" Certainly the convinced pluralist wouldn't think so!

Point # 2: We could offer an analogy from politics that does not bode well for the pluralist's point: "If you were born in Nazi Germany, you probably would have been one of the Hitler Youth." While this may be true, *does this mean that all political systems are equal?* Certainly not. Similarly, we may have good reason to believe a particular religion or worldview (outlook on life) to be true—regardless of what beliefs we grew up with. We may have good reason to *reject* another belief system—just as we have good reason to reject Nazism as a viable political option. For instance, if a belief-system is full of fundamental contradictions and philosophical flaws, then it should be rejected as false. If a belief-system has been explicitly founded on what turns out to be forged documents and flawed historical claims, then we are rightly justified in rejecting it. Moreover, one religion may offer a more plausible explanation for what we experience and for the facts we know than other religions can. So the issue at stake is rationality, not nationality!

Fifth, *we cannot stop with the examination of religious **practice** and **ritual** but must also deal with the **object** of religious belief.* Within the religious studies departments in universities around the United States (in which one might have a Christian, a Jew, a Muslim, a Buddhist, a Hindu, and even a shaman teaching courses), we observe a common tendency. Religious *experience* becomes the focal point, while truth-claims and matters of doctrinal differences between the various religions about the nature of the Ultimate Reality (e.g., whether God is personal or just some impersonal Principle) are obscured as a result.

Today people are into "spirituality"—be it Buddhist, Hindu, Christian; "religion," on the other hand, is associated with the musty and out-moded dimensions of doctrine, tradition, history, and creeds. This tendency, however, reduces religion to its lowest common denominator in the name of "harmony" and "cooperation," but the danger of this is that all discussion of *truth* is eliminated. But truth cannot really be truth *unless it excludes something*—namely, error and falsehood. While it may be quite informative to discuss and understand religious experiences and rituals throughout the world, we will be missing something terribly important if we do not move on to the topic of the *nature* of Ultimate Reality, the nature of the human problem, and what the solution to this problem is. And it is at this point that those "outmoded" and "worn-out" doctrines and historical realities can have a sta-bilizing as well as internally-transforming effect upon us.

Within the Christian faith, there are certain undeniable historical realities which, if false, would render Christianity completely unfound-ed and thus untrue. St. Paul said that if Jesus Christ has not been bodily raised from the dead, then we are believing a lie and we ought to be pitied (1 Corinthians 15:14, 17, 19). Paul is *not* saying, "Doesn't the Christian faith make us feel happy and contented? Doesn't it have a good effect upon those who believe it sincerely?" Paul says that if certain historical events and certain doctrinal beliefs turn out to be false, then those who would go on believing lies deserve pity, not praise. For the Christian, it is certain stable truths that give a foundation on which to build, a context to help us coherently interpret our experience in the world and make sense of it. Because of these truths, the Christian faith "works." (So the Christian faith is not just true because it works. After all, some false things can appear to "work"—even if for just a short time.)

It is ironic that people who claim to be "into" some brand of all-embracing "spirituality" are really just replacing one kind of exclusive "creed" for another. On the one hand, they don't want to enter into the "religious" world of truth and falsity, yet on the other hand, they believe that the "spiritual" perspective is the *correct* and *true* way of believing and the "religious" perspective is wrong-headed and should be rejected. For example, in his *Conversations With God*, Neale Walsch proclaims a creed of his own: "Listen to your feelings." "You have no obligations." "[The voice within] tells you whether everything else is true or false, right or wrong, good or bad as you have defined it." Feelings and intuitions should be trusted, not holy books or doctrines. But even though Walsch embraces "spirituality" and rejects "religion," Walsch still cannot escape absolute truths and "doctrines." For instance, he says (allegedly quoting God) that "words are the least reliable purveyor of truth." But if this is the case, *why should we take these words as being reliable purveyors of truth*? Walsch wants his reader to believe that the words he expresses not only in this sentence but in his books convey truth to the reader. Again we find that truth is *inescapable*. After all, Walsch clearly believes that his view is true and that those who would disagree with him are in error.

As I have thought about these important issues, I myself have come to see that the Christian faith has greater power to explain a broad range of human experience and knowledge than the alternatives:

• the origin of the universe with the Big Bang (which points to a prior cause, since something cannot come into existence, uncaused out of nothing);

• the delicate balance of cosmic conditions that make human life possible (e.g., if the rate of the universe's expansion were only slightly altered, life would be impossible);

• the affirmation of human dignity (which is more plausibly explained by our having been specially made by a personal God rather than by material processes that eventually produce intrinsically valuable beings—somehow!);

• the existence of consciousness (how could it emerge from purely non-conscious processes?);

• the existence of a world outside of my own mind, which I take to be true rather than illusory (as is commonly the case in some versions of Eastern religion and philosophy; but *why* reject what seems to be so obvious—namely, this world that exists—in favor of what appears to be clearly false: that the world is only an illusion?);

• the existence of objective moral values (e.g., what Mother Teresa did was really good, and what Adolf Hitler did was really evil)—a distinction which is rejected by some Eastern religious/philosophical systems because it pre-supposes that ultimate distinctions do not exist and that everything is One;

• the existence of real evil (which appears to presuppose the existence of some standard of goodness or of some kind of design plan, from which evil diverges);

• the unique claims of Jesus of Nazareth and the vindication of his claims by his bodily resurrection.[3]

Again, there **can** be good reasons for embracing one worldview or belief-system over another. We need not believe one way rather than another due to purely arbitrary reasons of where and when we happen to be born.[4]

Clearly, people's religious beliefs are influenced by different backgrounds, cultural baggage, and philosophical assumptions. But we must not mistakenly claim that there is no objective religious truth to be found. For if we did, then this claim itself would be an objective truth-claim about religion.

CONCLUSION

In closing, we must remember two things from our discussion: (a) *it's perfectly fine to* maintain that truth and falsity exist, that an objective reality exists, that moral right and wrong exist, and that some kind of exclusivism in religion exists. And the reason that this is perfectly fine is that (b) *objective truth is unavoidable*. After all, if we attempt to reject it, we'll do so on the basis of reasons we take to be true, and not false.

But if objective truth, reality, and morality exist, then this has certain implications for me. It means living in accordance with these truths rather than pretending they don't exist. It means resisting societal truth decay because this is the only reasonable alternative.

ENDNOTES

[1] For a popular, though brief, defense of the correspondence view of truth, see the booklet in this series by David Clark and James Beilby, *Why Bother With Truth?* For a more technical defense, see William P. Alston, *A Realist Conception of Truth* (Ithaca, N.Y.: Cornell University Press, 1996).

[2] For further defense of objective moral values, see Part II of my book "*True for You, But Not for Me.*" See also the booklet in this series that elaborates on this issue: Mark Linville, *Who Decides What's Right?*

[3] For further reading on this point, see Paul Copan, ed., *Will the Real Jesus Please Stand Up? A Debate Between William Lane Craig and John Dominic Crossan* (Grand Rapids: Baker, 1998); and Michael Wilkins and J.P. Moreland, eds., *Jesus Under Fire* (Grand Rapids: Zondervan, 1995). See also F.F. Bruce, *The New Testament Documents: Are They Reliable?* (Grand Rapids: Eerdmans, 1960); Colin Hemer, *The Book of Acts in the Setting of Hellenistic History* (Winona Lake, Ind.: Eisenbrauns, 1990).

[4] See William Craig's booklet in this RZIM Critical Questions series, *God, Are You There?*

SUGGESTED FURTHER READING

Beckwith, Francis and Koukl, Greg. *Relativism: Feet Firmly Planted in Mid-Air*. Grand Rapids: Baker, 1998. This book addresses the fundamental flaws of relativism. Especially helpful are its comments on the social, legal, and political ramifications of relativism. Popular-level.

Budziszewski, Jay. *How to Stay Christian in College: An Interactive Guide to Keeping the Faith*. Colorado Springs: Navpress, 1999. A useful tool for those in a university setting who are confronted with issues of relativism and "choosing" one's own morality. Popular-level.

Copan, Paul. *"True for You, But Not for Me": Deflating the Slogans That Leave Christians Speechless*. Minneapolis: Bethany House, 1998. This book deals with common slogans related to relativism, religious pluralism, the uniqueness of Christ, and the question of the unevangelized. Popular-level.

Kreeft, Peter. *A Refutation of Moral Relativism: Interviews with Absolutist.* Ft. Collins, Colo.: Ignatius, 1999. A series of entertaining fictitious interviews between a moral relativist and absolutist. Popular-level.

Nagel, Thomas. *The Last Word*. New York: Oxford University Press, 1997. Although this piece is written by an atheistic philosopher, it makes a forceful defense of objective truth. Advanced.

APPENDIX

BOOKLET IN A NUTSHELL:
A Summary of the Issues

Principle # 1:
RELATIVISM IS SELF-CONTRADICTORY

Truth is what corresponds or conforms to reality. And we tend to believe things because they are *true* rather than simply because our parents, friends, or culture tells us.

Relativism claims to be *absolutely* true. Consequently, because it is self-contradictory and therefore false, it should be rejected.

The relativist really believes that *relativism applies to everyone.* For instance, he believes that it applies to at least two people ("that's true for you, but not for me") and not simply himself.

Just because differences exist, this does not prove that relativism is true. In fact, the *basis* for holding to relativism (that many people disagree) is at least *true—not false*; and the relativist's conclusion about the inevitability of relativism is also taken to be *true—not false*.

Those who say that trying to "convert" others is wrong (and absolutely wrong!) are often trying to convert others to *their* point of view.

If it is arrogant to believe in objective truth, then people on *both* sides are arrogant.

Arrogance, however, deals primarily with *attitudes* rather than *beliefs*. (And the Christian's attitude should be like that of one beggar's telling another where to find bread.)

It's *perfectly fine* to believe in objective truth—especially since objective truth is inescapable anyway!

Principle # 2:
REALITY IS OBJECTIVE

No matter how much we think we shape reality, at some point we must admit that some of our very own beliefs (like the assumption that we can create *any* reality we want) are themselves *immune* to human manipulation.

And no matter how strong may be the influence of genetics or cultural environment upon us, we still possess at least *some* objectivity in order to draw conclusions about the strength of these influences

Even though our thinking is limited by many factors, this does not mean we cannot achieve *some* objectivity.

To believe that (a) **we all can shape reality any way we choose** (the wet lump of clay image) is to believe that there is at least *one* reality we cannot shape or manipulate—namely, that we can all shape our own reality. Those who claim that reality is nothing more than a wet lump of clay believe that this view pertains to *all* people—not just themselves.

Furthermore, the idea that *believing sincerely* makes something true is self-contradictory. After all, what if I *sincerely believe* that simply believing *does not* make something true? Besides, none of us really lives this way in the everyday life of traffic jams, financial concerns, and social problems. Sincerely believing otherwise will not make them go away.

The conclusion people draw that (b) **reality is shaped for us by factors independent of us** (such as genetics, history, culture, language) is *itself* not thought to be the product of those influences but objective and independent of them. Those who conclude this don't *really* believe this about their own views! (For example, historians who claim that there is no difference between fiction and non-fiction in history believe that theirs is *not* a fictitious assertion!)

The belief that everything is *perspectival* (like an "opinion") is asserted as though this is *true* for everyone and *not false* and that there are *reasons* for believing this to be the case (reasons which are true and not false).

Those who reduce all that we think and do to genetics, environment, reproduction and survival, or language do one of two things: (a) they *contradict themselves* by acting as though they have escaped the influences everyone else is subject to (the self-excepting fallacy); or (b) they *say nothing at all* since what they express is nothing more than the product of those influences.

Principle #3:
LOGIC IS NOT ARBITRARY

To deny the validity of logic (e.g., "that's just Western logic"), we will end up *using* logic in order to do so.

Logic is necessary for language, not the other way around. Even the distinction between words in a sentence presupposes the logical law of non-contradiction ("A does not equal non-A").

Principle # 4:
MAKING JUDGMENTS IS INEVITABLE

If we think one should never "judge" but then point out that *others* are "judging," we ourselves have just *made a judgment*.

When people say, "Who are you to judge?", *ask* what they mean by "judge." And aren't they judging *you* for judging *someone* else?

Remember that there are good judgments and bad judgments. An example of *wrongful* judgment (*judgmentalism*) is in Matthew 7:1, in which one feels *morally superior* or smug in light of the failure of others. But there is also a *proper* kind of judgment we can make (e.g., John 7:24) that is, it is not superficial but accurate.

Principle # 5:
TOLERANCE MUST BE CLARIFIED

When called "intolerant," we must first ask: "What do you mean by *tolerance*?"

The "tolerance" which "accepts all views as true or legitimate" will be self-contradictory. (The person who calls you "intolerant" does not accept *your* view as true!)

True tolerance, as historically understood, recognizes the difference between *persons*, who should be treated with respect, and the *beliefs* they hold, with which we need not agree.

Relativists tend to treat "tolerance" as an absolute: "You can believe whatever you want— *only* be tolerant of other beliefs." (Presumably it is universally *wrong* to be intolerant!)

We must balance convictions and truth with civility and graciousness. We must speak the truth in love (Ephesians 4:10).

Principle # 6:
MORAL RELATIVISM IS UNLIVABLE

This means that people *really* do think it is wrong to violate their rights, and even relativists get *upset* and *offended* at the apparent "immorality" of moral absolutes.

Those who get upset at "imposing" morality on others apparently believe that it is *morally wrong* to impose morality on others. But why get so uptight if everything is relative?

There are objective moral facts (Nazi or Stalinist brutalities, widow burning, torture). We intuitively recognize such truths as "torturing babies for fun is wrong"; "murder or theft is wrong"; "kindness is good." There seems no good reason to reject these intuitions.

To say that another culture's practices are *immoral* is not cultural arrogance if there is the recognition of moral flaws within one's own culture (as well as the virtues within other cultures).

To assume that one culture cannot "make judgments" about another actually undermines the possibility of moral reform (e.g., abolishing slave trade, civil rights for minorities).

Moral relativism is *unlivable*. Many are simply *selective* about which moral truths they live by: they believe that cheating on exams or sexual freedom is all right, but it's wrong for others to steal from *them* or violate *their* rights.

Principle # 7:
RELIGIOUS PLURALISM
IS EXCLUSIVISTIC

If someone believes all religions lead to salvation or liberation, he believes he has a virtue that persons within a particular religious tradition do not have: He believes he is right and traditional religious adherents are not. Pluralism is therefore *exclusivistic* in that it takes a "God's eye-view" on religious matters.

If religious beliefs are simply culturally-conditioned responses to the Ultimate Reality, then religious pluralism is just another one of those culturally-conditioned responses. Yet the religious pluralist gives the impression that his own view is not culturally conditioned. (He acts as the *observer* of the blind men touching the elephant—and *not* one of the blind men!).

All religions are exclusivistic, not just Christianity (e.g., Buddha rejected the Vedic scriptures of Hinduism and its belief in the enduring soul). All religions are characterized by taking a certain "God's eye-view" of things.

To emphasize religious *experience* and *practice* and ignore the *object* of religion and doctrinal truths is to evade what all systems—whether that of "religion" or "spirituality"—must face. *Why* should I believe what I do if there is no reason to think it is *true* rather than false?

The *rationality* of belief is more important than the *geography* of belief. Just because we were born in a certain religious environment does not entail the truth of religious pluralism. (Think of the question: "What if you had grown up in Nazi Germany?") Rather, are there *good reasons* for accepting one belief system over against another? Which viewpoint has the best explanatory power? This is the more fundamental matter since it deals with objective and non-arbitrary factors.

PROJECTED BOOKLETS IN THE RZIM
CRITICAL QUESTIONS SERIES

William Craig, *God, Are You There? Five Reasons God Exists and Three Reasons It Makes a Difference* (available)

Paul Copan, *Is Everything Really Relative? Examining the Assumptions of Relativism and the Culture of Truth Decay* (available)

Scott Armstrong, *Who's Shaping My Life? Assessing the Media's Influence on Our Culture*

Darrell Bock, *Can I Trust the Bible? Defending the Bible's Reliability*

David K. Clark and James Beilby, *Why Bother With Truth? Arriving at Knowledge in a Skeptical Society*

Douglas Geivett, *Can a Good God Allow Evil? Making Sense of Suffering*

Klaus Issler, *What Does It Mean To Be Human? Understanding Who We Really Are*

Mark Linville, *Who Decides What's Right? Defending Objective Morality*

L. T. Jeyachandran *Does the East Have the Answers? Getting Perspective on Eastern Religion and Philosophy*

Stuart McAllister, *Born to Shop? Exposing the Threat of a Consumer Culture*

Paul K. Moser, *Why Doesn't God Make Himself More Obvious? Understanding the God Who Hides and Seeks*

Michael Ramsden, *What's the Point? Finding Meaning and Hope in God*

John Mark Reynolds, *Do the Bible and Science Conflict? Reconciling the Differences*

Ravi Zacharias, *What's So Special About Jesus? Encountering Christ Among the World's Religions*

OTHER PROJECTED TITLES

Is the Bible Historically Reliable? Examining the Historical and Archaeological Evidence

Isn't the God of the Bible Cruel and Vindictive? Understanding Ethical Issues in the Bible

If you have further questions or are in need of additional resources, please contact Ravi Zacharias International Ministries, 4725 Peachtree Corners Circle, Suite 250, Norcross, Georgia 30092.

Order line: 800.448.6766
Fax: 770.729.1729
E-mail: rzim@rzim.com
Website: http://www.gospelcom.net/rzim/

RZIM is a ministry founded by Dr. Ravi Zacharias with the goal to reach and challenge those who shape the ideas of a culture with the credibility of the message of Jesus Christ.

If you are interested in obtaining a first-rate philosophical journal written with articles written by leading Christian philosophers, we encourage you to subscribe to *Philosophia Christi*, the journal of the Evangelical Philosophical Society (EPS). Please contact:

Craig Hazen
Biola University
13800 Biola Ave
La Mirada, CA 90639-0001
562.903.6000

Or check out the EPS website at http://www.epsociety.org

Published by RZIM
Ravi Zacharias International Ministries
4725 Peachtree Corners Circle, Suite 250
Norcross, Georgia 30092
HYPERLINK http://www.gospelcom.net/rzim/   http://www.gospelcom.net/rzim/

Library of Congress Cataloging-in-Publication Data

Copan, Paul 1999
Is Everything Really Relative? / Examining the Assumptions of Relativism and the Culture of Truth Decay.

ISBN 1-930107-01-3

1. Apologetics.   2. Relativity-Controversial Literature.
4. Contemporary Issues   5. Christianity-Philosophy.

I AM RESPONSIBLE:
The Hand of AA

᠅

II